W9-BOB-291

Senses in the City
Shelley Rotner

M Millbrook Press   Minneapolis

To Jean,
with gratitude for having the vision to see
my books through as I would.

Millbrook Press
A division of Lerner Publishing Group, Inc.
241 First Avenue North
Minneapolis, MN U.S.A. 55401

Website address: www.lernerbooks.com

Library of Congress Cataloging-in-Publication Data

Rotner, Shelley.
    Senses in the city / by Shelley Rotner.
       p.   cm. — (Shelley Rotner's early childhood library)
    ISBN 978-0-8225-7502-3 (lib. bdg. : alk. paper)
    1. Senses and sensation—Juvenile literature.   2. Cities and towns—
Juvenile literature.   I. Title.
QP434.R66 2008
612.8—dc22   2007021887

Manufactured in the United States of America
1 2 3 4 5 6 – DP – 13 12 11 10 09 08

In the city . . .

See the city skyline and the bridge.

Touch the elevator button

. . .and the escalator railing.

Hear
the sirens

. . . and the traffic.

Smell
the flowers at
a corner store.

Taste a giant, warm pretzel.

See the murals.

Touch
the pole in the subway car.

Hear
a train passing by.

Taste special foods from all over the world.

Smell the ripe fruit at a street stand.

See the tall buildings.

Hear
the musicians
playing to a
crowd.

Taste a cookie from a neighborhood bakery.

Smell the fish at the local market.

See
the dolphins
at the science
museum . . .

or the birds on
the city streets.

Taste
cool water from the fountain.

Touch the metal parking meter.

Smell the garbage on pickup day.

Hear
the jackhammer
at a construction
site.

Taste
sweet treats from
the candy store.

Touch
hands to cross a busy street.

See the city lights at night.

In the city, there's so much to

see,   hear,   smell,   taste,   touch.